ICEBERGS
AND
GLACIERS

SEYMOUR SIMON

SCHOLASTIC INC.

New York   Toronto   London   Auckland   Sydney
Mexico City   New Delhi   Hong Kong

PICTURE CREDITS

TERRAPHOTOGRAPHICS/B PS /B. F. Molnia, pages 7, 9, 13, 16, 17, 18 (both), 19, 20, 21, 30, 32; NASA, pages 14, 23; Nikon/Lisa Winston-Pontaski, page 6; Charles Swithinbank, pages 4, 24, 25, 26, 27, cover; U.S. Coast Guard, page 29; U.S. Geological Survey, page 11. Drawings on page 10 by Warren Budd.

ISBN 0-439-18021-X

12 11 10 9 8 7 6 5   1 2 3 4 5/0

Printed in the U.S.A.   09

First Scholastic printing, February 2000

To my new friends in Ketchikan, Alaska

For most of us, spring means the return of warm weather. Snows melt and frozen lakes and rivers thaw. The icy scenes of winter begin to disappear.

But some places are cold all year round. This photo was taken at midnight during the middle of summer in Antarctica. At that time of year, the sun never sets during the night but remains low in the sky.

Antarctica is always covered by deep layers of ice and snow. So, too, are parts of Greenland, Canada, Alaska, and Iceland. Even when summer comes, ice and snow cover about one-tenth of Earth's land surface.

The upper slopes and peaks of high mountains all over the world are also covered by ice and snow. These places of everlasting snow are said to be above the snow line. Summertime snow fields are found in the Rockies, the Himalayas, the Alps, the Andes, and even at the equator high atop Mount Kilimanjaro. It is in the constantly cold lands and above the snow line that glaciers are born.

A single snowflake is a feathery crystal of ice about the size of your fingernail. Every snowflake is six-sided, yet each has a different shape.

Once the spinning flakes fall to the ground, they begin to clump together and lose their pointed beauty. Soon the snowflakes become rounded grains of ice with tiny bubbles of air trapped inside. As more snow falls, the weight of the snow and ice squeezes the grains of ice together, forcing out the trapped air. The color of the ice begins to change, too. The white of airy snow becomes the steel blue of airless ice. Finally, the blue ice crystals begin to pack together into a solid field of ice.

As more snow falls, the ice field becomes thicker and heavier, pressing downward with great force against the ground. As years go by, the ice field grows until it is about sixty feet deep. Then something strange happens.

The huge mass of ice begins to move. The ice bends and cracks and begins to slide over the ground, moving downhill. The ice moves slowly, usually less than two feet a day and sometimes only an inch or two. But however slowly, when an ice field begins to move, it has become a glacier.

Glaciers are sometimes called rivers of ice, but a glacier moves differently than a river. Water flows freely but ice is hard and can crack easily. For many years, scientists called glaciologists have studied how glaciers move. Some of their early findings were accidental. In 1827, one Swiss scientist built a hut on an Alpine glacier. When he returned three years later, he found that the hut had moved more than one hundred yards downhill.

In recent years, scientists have found that glaciers move in two different ways. One way is by sliding across the ground on a very thin film of water from melted ice. This meltwater, sometimes only the thickness of a page in this book, allows the ice to slide more easily.

The second way that a glacier moves is called "creep." The tremendous weight of the glacier makes the crystals of ice slowly form layers one atop another. Then the layers begin gliding or creeping over one another.

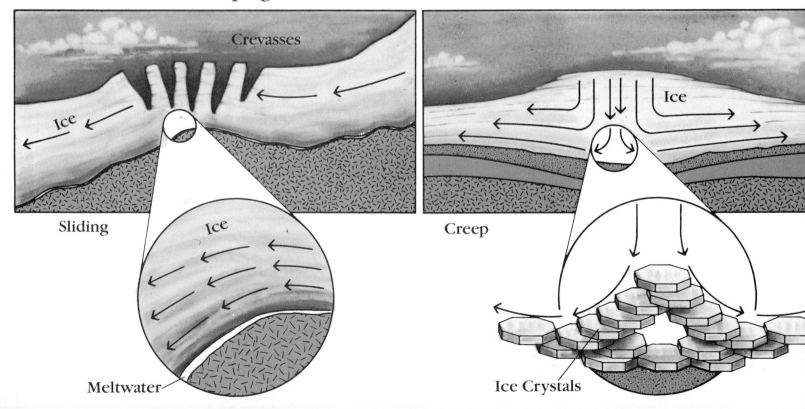

Sliding

Meltwater

Creep

Ice Crystals

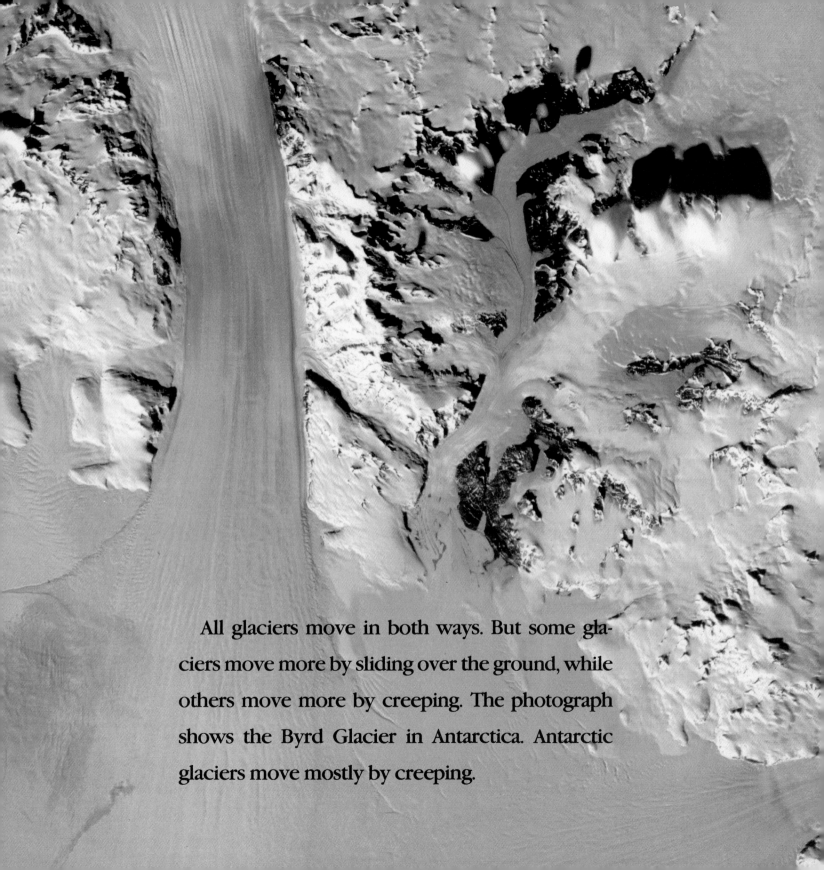

All glaciers move in both ways. But some glaciers move more by sliding over the ground, while others move more by creeping. The photograph shows the Byrd Glacier in Antarctica. Antarctic glaciers move mostly by creeping.

Different parts of a glacier move at different speeds. Louis Agassiz, a nineteenth-century Swiss naturalist and scientist, once planted rows of stakes in straight lines across a glacier. The following year Agassiz found that the stakes had all moved down the valley. But the stakes in the middle of the glacier had moved the farthest. That showed that the ice in the middle of the glacier was moving faster than the ice along the sides.

In the early part of the twentieth century, Swiss and Italian scientists drilled holes straight down through the thickness of a glacier. Then they placed iron rods in the holes. Over the years, the scientists found that the rods bent at the top. This showed that the ice at the top of a glacier moves more quickly than the ice at the bottom.

Nowadays, glaciologists use photography and other methods to learn about glaciers. The photo shows a scientist using an instrument called a transit to help find out the speed of a glacier.

The thicker the glacier the faster it moves. That's because the greater weight of the glacier causes the crystals of ice to creep more rapidly. Also, a steep glacier will flow much more quickly than one on level land.

Temperature is a third factor that affects the speed of a glacier. The warmer the glacier the faster the ice moves because there is a greater amount of meltwater beneath the ice. In fact, scientists sometimes group glaciers together depending upon whether they are cold or warm. But even "warm" glaciers are still freezing.

Some glaciers move so slowly that you might not notice their movement for a long time. The cold Alaskan glaciers in this aerial photo creep downhill at only about six inches per *year*. But there are some steep, warm glaciers that flow more than one hundred feet a *day*.

As the glacier moves, the ice on top bends and sometimes cracks. The cracks in the ice are called crevasses. The crevasses can be deep and wide and very dangerous. This group of scientists exploring the Juneau Ice Field in Canada has to travel carefully.

When glaciers move, they grind and crush everything in their path. Small stones and huge rocks are pulled from the ground and carried along. Slowly, but with irresistible force, glaciers cut and carve the land. Trees, forests, hills, and even mountains are ground down over the years. The photo shows how most of the mountain has been carried away by the ice, leaving sharp peaks and ragged ridges.

As glaciers move, they often scratch lines into the layers of rock that lie beneath the soil. The scratches are made by smaller rocks carried along by the ice.

Sometimes glaciers wear down the bedrock to smooth, rounded humps. To some people, these rocks have the shapes of a flock of grazing sheep. So they are called *roches moutonnées*, French words that mean "sheep rocks."

The rocks carried along by a glacier are broken down and ground into smaller and smaller pieces. The smaller pieces are ground again and again until they are very tiny particles, almost too small for you to see. These particles, called rock flour, are carried away by a glacier's meltwater. The rock flour carried by the meltwater stream from a glacier has turned the seawater a grayish brown color.

Not all of the rocks carried by a glacier are ground into rock flour. Some of the rocks are left behind along the edges or at the end of a glacier. Sometimes these rocks build up into ridges or piles called moraines. You can see the moraines in this photo of the Worthington Glacier in Alaska.

There are many different kinds of glaciers. Mountain glaciers start in snowfields atop mountains. Then they begin to move downward following valleys until they reach the snow line and melt during the summer.

Mountain glaciers are often thousands of feet wide and many miles long. Avalanches of snow roar down their surfaces.

Sometimes mountain glaciers do not melt when they reach the bottom of the mountain. Instead, the glaciers flow over the countryside to form ice fields over the level ground.

Bigger than most mountain glaciers are ice caps —mountain glaciers that have become so thick that the mountain is almost buried. This computer-colored photo of Iceland was taken by satellite. The red spots are hot, active volcanoes. The green and the yellow areas are places where the temperatures are medium. The smaller white spots are mountain glaciers. The large white areas are ice caps.

Iceland's largest ice cap covers more than three thousand square miles. There is an active volcano buried beneath the western part of that ice cap. The heat from the volcano is always melting the ice above, forming a huge reservoir of meltwater. Every five years or so, the meltwater bursts out from under an edge of the cap. The roaring waters carry large boulders and giant blocks of ice. For miles around, the land is flooded and becomes a vast lake.

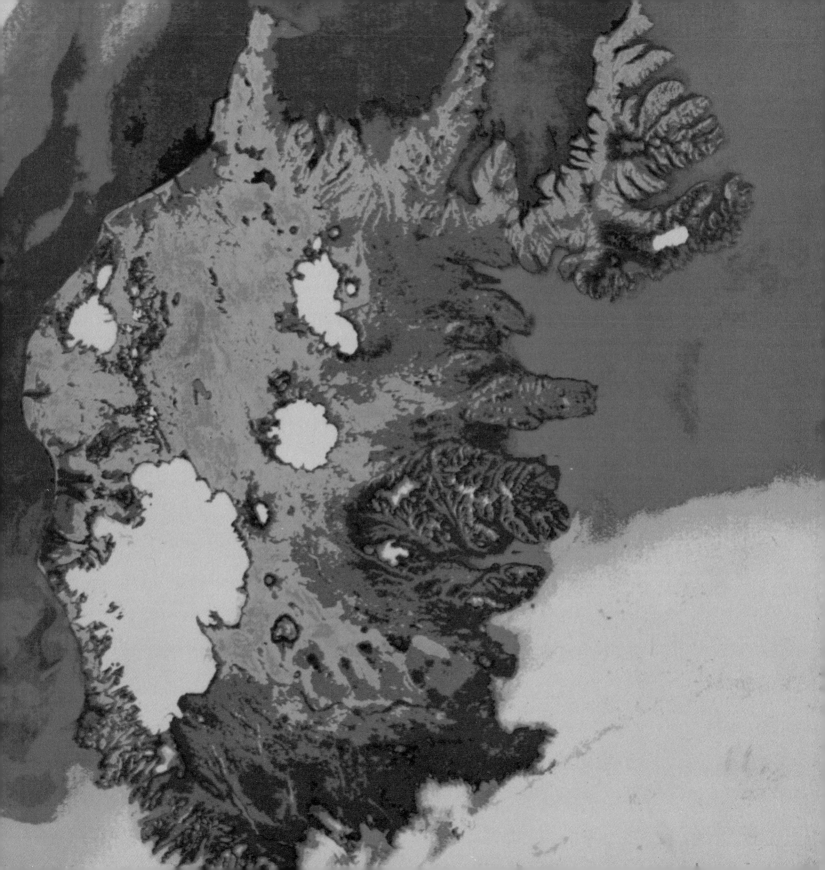

Ice sheets are the largest kind of glaciers. The Antarctic ice sheet is the biggest in the world. It is larger than the United States, Mexico, and Central America combined. In some places, the Antarctic ice sheet is more than fifteen thousand feet thick. That's about the height of ten Empire State Buildings stacked one atop another. Where an ice sheet meets the sea, it forms an ice shelf over the water.

Large masses of ice often break away from glaciers or ice shelves. The glacier is said to be calving, and the floating blocks of ice are called icebergs.

The icebergs in the photo are eighty to one hundred feet high and several miles long. Each is a floating island of ice. The largest iceberg ever measured was about two hundred miles long and sixty miles wide. That's bigger than the state of Vermont or the country of Belgium.

As an iceberg floats, it melts, changes shape, and breaks apart. Until an iceberg melts and disappears completely, most of it is underwater.

Only a small part of an iceberg shows above the water. About seven-eighths of the "berg" is hidden beneath the waves because glacial ice is slightly lighter than an equal amount of seawater. The large unseen part of an iceberg adds to the danger of a collision with a nearby ship.

On the night of April 14, 1912, the *Titanic*, the "safest ship in the world" according to its builders, was steaming across the North Atlantic. Yet in a few hours the ship had gone to the bottom of the ocean after striking a large iceberg. More than fifteen hundred people died in the icy waters that night. The next year, the International Ice Patrol was established, and it is still on the job. The patrol searches for dangerous icebergs and helps ships avoid them.

In the future, icebergs may prove to be useful as a source of fresh water for dry lands. One plan calls for mile-long Antarctic icebergs to be towed to distant countries by powerful tugboats and helicopters. The icebergs would be wrapped

with layers of plastic insulation to protect them from melting on their journey. But there are still many problems with this idea, and it may be many years, if ever, before icebergs are transported in this way.

Twenty thousand years ago, ice sheets covered most of Canada, all of New England, and much of the midwestern and northwestern United States. Most of Great Britain and large parts of the Soviet Union, Germany, and Poland, along with smaller parts of Austria, Italy, and France, were also covered by ice. Then, about ten thousand years ago, the ice began to melt. Today glaciers are found only in cold polar regions and high mountains.

During the past million years, glaciers and ice sheets have advanced and covered large parts of the earth at least four times and perhaps as many as ten times. Scientists call this period of time the Pleistocene ice ages. (Pleistocene comes from Greek words that mean "most recent.")

Today we can see the ways that the land was changed by the glaciers. The rivers of ice cut valleys through the land and made rolling hills. Rocks and boulders were dragged from one place and dropped in other places far away.

Perhaps the place where you live now was once covered by ice. If you look around, you may find clues to past ice ages: scratches on bedrock, a big boulder that stands alone, a round pond left behind as the ice melted.

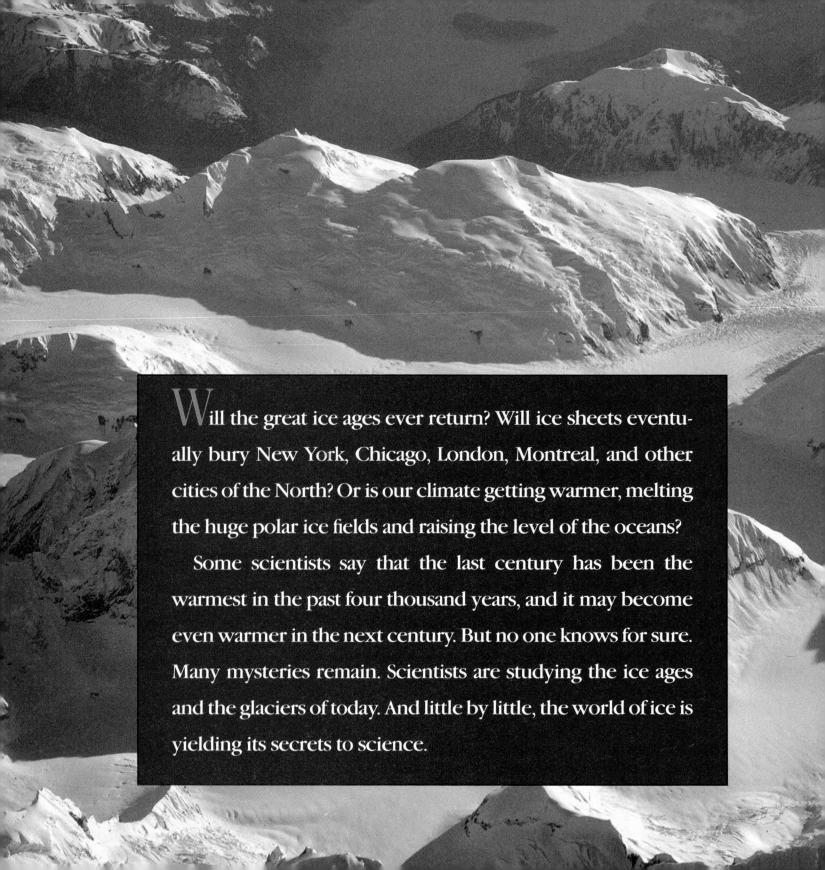

Will the great ice ages ever return? Will ice sheets eventually bury New York, Chicago, London, Montreal, and other cities of the North? Or is our climate getting warmer, melting the huge polar ice fields and raising the level of the oceans?

Some scientists say that the last century has been the warmest in the past four thousand years, and it may become even warmer in the next century. But no one knows for sure. Many mysteries remain. Scientists are studying the ice ages and the glaciers of today. And little by little, the world of ice is yielding its secrets to science.